SHADOWS

SHADOWS

Here, There, and Everywhere

Ron & Nancy Goor

HarperCollins*Publishers*

Library of Congress Cataloging in Publication Data

Goor, Ron.
Shadows: here, there, and everywhere.
Summary: Presents information about shadows,
including how they are formed, why they can be
of various lengths, and how they reveal the
shape and texture of things.
1. Shades and shadows—Juvenile literatuure.
[1. Shadows] I. Goor, Nancy. II. Title.
QC381.6G66 1981   535′.4   81-43036
ISBN 0-690-04132-2   AACR2 ISBN 0-690-04133-0 (lib. bdg.)

6 7 8 9 10

This book is dedicated to shadows everywhere,
and especially to those of Daniel and Alex

Shadows are everywhere. Look around you. 7

Shadows can be big or small.

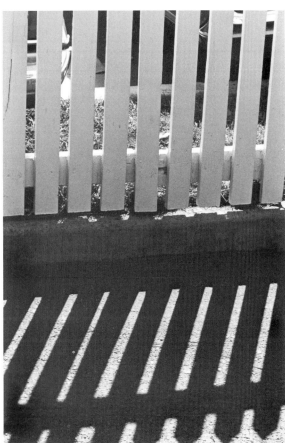

They can be fancy or plain.

Shadows can be long or short.

And sometimes shadows can be scary.

What makes a shadow?
Light…
an object…
a surface.

Shine a light on a wall in a darkened room. Place your hand in the ray of light.

The light goes around your hand. The light goes between your fingers. But the light cannot go through your hand. The light shines on the wall except where your hand blocks out the light and makes a shadow.

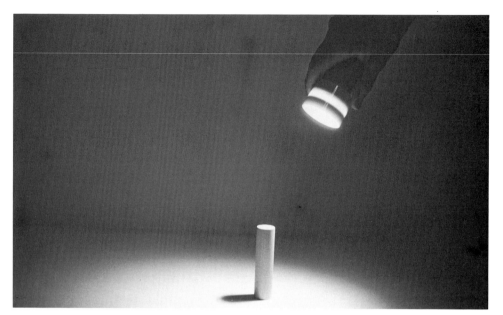

Change the position of the light and the shadow changes.

When the light is high, the shadow is short. At midday when the sun is high in the sky, shadows are short and fat.

When the light is low, the shadow is long. Early in the morning and late in the afternoon, when the sun is low in the sky, shadows are long and thin.

Change the number of lights and the number of shadows change. When two lights shine on you, you have two shadows.

How many lights are shining on the ballerina? On
the ice skaters?

Change the position of the object and the shadow
changes.

Every object has many different shadows. 19

Change the object and the shadow changes.

Objects with different shapes have different
shadows.

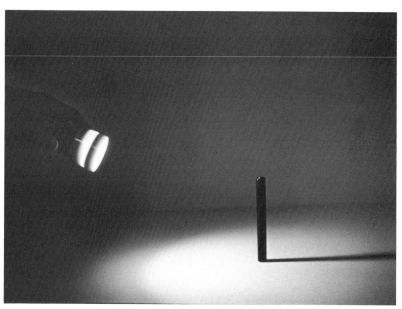

Change the surface and the shadow changes. The
shadow is flat when the surface is flat.

The shadow zigs and zags as it bends around corners and up and down steps. What happens to the shadow when the surface curves?

Can there be light, an object, and a surface but no shadow? When a larger object blocks the light from shining on a smaller object, the smaller object has no shadow.

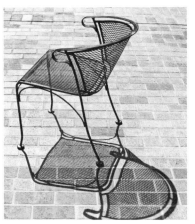

On cloudy days shadows are hard to find. This is because water particles in the air scatter the sun's light. In which picture of the chair has the sun gone behind a cloud? Are the children playing soccer on a sunny day or an overcast day?

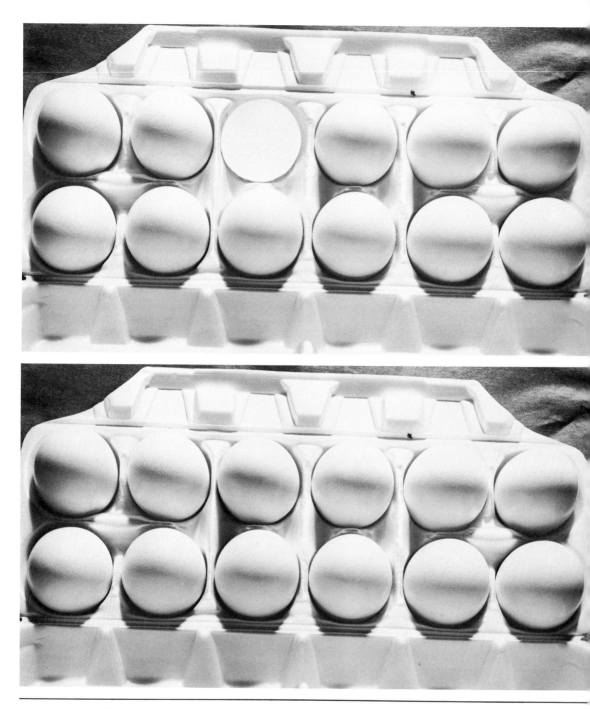

Shadows are useful. They help you know what shapes things have.

Without the delicate shadow on an egg, the egg would look flat—like a flat circle. Can you find the egg with the missing shadow?

What helps you see the shape of the Washington Monument?

Shadows help you know if things are rough or smooth.

When the sun shines on the side of this tree, the bark appears rough. The long shadow of each piece of bark shows us the texture of the tree. When the sun shines directly on the tree, there are no shadows on the bark. The bark looks smoother.

Is this a ball or an orange? How do you know? 29

People use shadows to tell time. See how the long shadow on the sundial lies between IX (9:00) and X (10:00). It is 9:30. In half an hour, the shadow will have moved to X (10:00). As the sun moves across the sky, the sundial shadow moves across the dial and marks the time.

Does the sundial tell time at night?
On cloudy days?

Shadows can shade you from the sun. Trees, hats,
and umbrellas make shadows that keep you cool.

Shadows can also be fun.

You can play games with your shadow. Try making the eagle, the duck, the clown, and the hawk. Can you make them move? What other shadow puppets can you make?

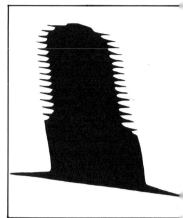

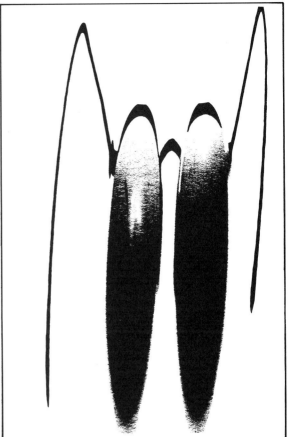

Look carefully at these shadows. Can you guess what object is making the shadow? With some of the shadows it is hard to tell. Turn the page to find the answers.

Fork

Screw

Toothbrush

Plant

Shopping cart

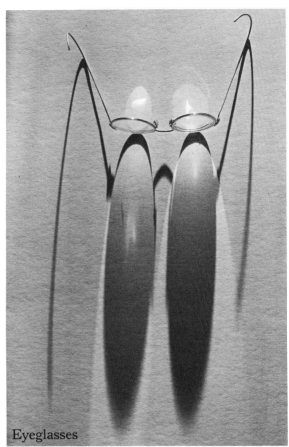

Eyeglasses

Railing

Shadows can be fun. You can play games with them.

Shadows are useful. They show us shape and texture. They keep us cool. They can show us the time.

Shadows can be beautiful and interesting.

Shadows can be big or small.

Shadows can be long or short or fancy or plain.　　43

Look around you.

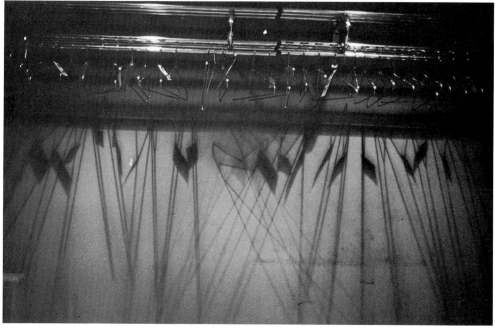

Shadows are everywhere.

Ron Goor was born and raised in Washington, D.C. He was graduated from Swarthmore College and attended the University of Chicago and Harvard University, where he received a Master's degree in public health and a Ph.D. in biochemistry.

Nancy Goor also grew up in Washington, D.C. A graduate of the University of Pennsylvania, she received her M.F.A. from Boston University.

Together, the Goors conceived, designed, and directed the first live insect zoo at the Smithsonian's Natural History Museum. *Shadows: Here, There, and Everywhere* is their first book for children.

The Goors live in Bethesda, Maryland, with their two sons, Alexander and Daniel.